SIXTY SECOND SCIENCE

100 SCIENCE
MYSTERIES EXPLAINED

Managing Editor:
Simon Melhuish

Series Editor:
Nikole G. Bamford

Design & Layout:
Linley J. Clode

Compilers and Checkers:
Nick Daws
Tom Melhuish

Published by The Lagoon Group
UK: PO Box 311, KT2 5QW, UK.
US: 10685-B Hazelhurst Dr. #9988,
Houston, TX 77043, USA.

© The Lagoon Group.
All rights reserved. No part of this
publication may be reproduced, stored
in a retrieval system, or transmitted
in any form or by any other means,
electronic, mechanical, photocopying or
otherwise, without prior permission in
writing from the publisher.

Printed in China

ISBN: 978-1-907780-08-0

www.thelagoongroup.com

INTRODUCTION

WHY IS THE SKY BLUE?

WHY DOES A BEE DIE AFTER STINGING, BUT A WASP DOESN'T?

WHY DOESN'T AN EXPANDING POPULATION MAKE OUR WORLD ANY HEAVIER?

These are the fundamental mysteries of life. We think we know the answers, but do we really?

In a spectacular mix of simple explanations and scientific facts this book answers 100 of the world's most intriguing and interesting questions.

You will be able to amaze your friends and enlighten inquisitive kids. Embrace your inner Einstein.

SIXTY
SECOND
SCIENCE

Why is the sky blue?

Most people think the sky is blue because it reflects the sea but actually, during the day, the sky appears blue because of the way sunlight is scattered within the atmosphere.

Light from the sun is actually white. When it reaches our planet's atmosphere, some of it is absorbed by the gas molecules there. After a while, the molecules release the light in a different direction. The color that is radiated is the same color that was absorbed.

The different colors of light are affected differently. All colors can be absorbed, but the higher frequencies (blues) are absorbed more often than the lower frequencies (reds). This process is called Rayleigh scattering, named after Lord John Rayleigh, the English physicist who first described it.

The sky appears blue because of this Rayleigh scattering. Because more blue light is absorbed and then radiated in different directions by gases in the atmosphere, whichever way you look some blue light reaches you. Since you see blue light from everywhere overhead, the sky looks blue.

At sunset, light from the sun must travel further through the atmosphere before it reaches your eyes. Even more of the higher-frequency blues and greens are scattered away as a result. Only the lower frequencies are left in the direct beam that reaches your eyes, which is why a setting sun looks yellow or red.

02 Why do you laugh when you're tickled?

It's generally believed that we laugh when tickled because of the surprise and the release of tension.

Laughter is often associated with the build-up and release of tension. In the children's game of hide-and-seek, for example, tension builds due to the uncertainty of what we will find when we search in a particular place. The sudden release of tension when we find the person hiding is typically marked by laughter.

With tickling, the laughter is caused not only by the surprise of the initial 'attack', but also by our uncertainty over what the tickler will do next. This creates tension, which is then released through laughter. The reason we don't laugh when we tickle ourselves is because our brain already knows what is going to happen, so there is no surprise, and no release of tension occurs.

So if we laugh when we are tickled, it doesn't necessarily mean that we find the tickling amusing. Rather, it's an involuntary reaction to the surprise and tension caused by the actions of the tickler.

03 Can carrots really help your night vision?

Carrots contain a substance called beta-carotene (did you notice the 'carot' in that?), which is turned by the body into Vitamin A.

Lack of Vitamin A can cause poor vision, including night vision. In such cases, eating more carrots will provide extra Vitamin A and help your night vision improve.

Most people eating a nutritious, balanced diet today will not be deficient in Vitamin A, so the benefits they will gain to their eyesight from eating carrots are limited. Millions of people in the developing world are, however, believed to suffer from Vitamin A deficiency.

There is an urban legend that eating large amounts of carrots will let you see in the dark. This developed from stories of British airmen in World War Two, who were able to shoot down German planes in the darkness of night. The RAF circulated a story about their pilots eating lots of carrots as an attempt to cover up the discovery and use of radar and other technology. It reinforced existing German folklore, and helped encourage Britons – looking to improve their night vision during the blackouts – to grow and eat the vegetable.

Carrots really are very good for you, and they may improve your night vision in the event that you aren't getting enough Vitamin A in your diet. But no amount of carrots will give you X-ray eyes.

04 Why do we have fingerprints?

Many an old-fashioned detective story has revolved around a set of tell-tale fingerprints left at the scene of the crime. And, of course, it's true that every one of us has a unique set of 'dabs', a fact which has been used by law enforcement officers to identify criminals since ancient times.

One popular theory as to why we have fingerprints is that they help us grip better. However, recent scientific studies have cast doubt on this. A 2009 UK study showed that fingerprints actually reduced friction when a flat, dry surface (perspex) was slid across the skin of the fingertips.

Another suggestion is that fingerprints improve our sense of touch by fine-tuning the information we pick up from surfaces. In one recent study in France, scientists investigated this idea by performing a series of experiments with artificial fingertips made with rubber-like sensors. They compared the sensitivity between these grooved artificial fingertips and a smooth skin-like material. They found that the grooved fingertips produced vibrations up to 100 times stronger than the smooth material when sliding against a roughened surface. The researchers suggested that the increased vibrations from fingerprints may enhance our sense of touch, especially for detecting textures.

Overall, though, it's clear that the function of fingerprints still needs a bit of detective work...

If you put a banana in the fridge, the skin will go brown, then black, much faster. The actual fruit inside won't ripen any faster, though.

The reason this happens is that the cold temperature in the fridge encourages an enzyme naturally found in the banana named polyphenyl oxidase to convert chemicals called phenols in the banana skin into polyphenols. Polyphenols are similar to melanin, the pigment responsible for the color in our skin. This is what darkens the skin of the bananas.

Despite the color, the cold temperature will keep your banana firmer then a banana that was left at room temperature for the same amount of time. The enzymes that break the starch into sugar (which makes the banana soft and ripe) work better at room temperature.

If you want to store ripe or almost-ripe bananas, they will last several days longer if you put them in the vegetable crisper drawer of your fridge. You can even store ripe bananas in your freezer. Once they are defrosted they are a bit mushy, but great for making smoothies or banana bread.

But if you have a fridge-blackened banana, please don't just assume it's 'bad' and throw it away – chances are, the fruit inside will still be delicious.

Many sports, from swimming to skiing, require you to wear goggles to protect your eyes. If they fog up, not only can you no longer see properly, but you are more likely to suffer (or cause) an accident. Anti-fogging goggles are therefore an important safety tool.

Fogging is caused by water vapor condensing on the inside of your goggles in tiny droplets. This vapor comes mainly from your perspiration evaporating. Obviously, if you are doing something strenuous such as skiing, you are likely to work up a good sweat.

Anti-fogging goggles have a thin layer of special coating applied to the inside. This prevents water vapor condensing in the tiny droplets that cause fogging. Anti-fogging coatings work by minimizing the surface tension in the water. As a result, instead of thousands of tiny droplets, the water vapor condenses as a thin film of water, an effect called wetting. This may still be irritating inside your goggles, but at least you can see through it.

As well as buying anti-fogging goggles, you can also buy special sprays, gels or wipes to treat ordinary ones. These normally work well, but the treatment has to be reapplied regularly. At a pinch, wiping your goggles with saliva (spit) can help reduce fogging – with the added benefit that nobody else will want to borrow them after you've done so.

07 How does wearing dark clothing make you look thinner?

It's true that dark clothes make you look thinner, with black being the most slimming of them all. That's presumably why every woman has a little black dress somewhere in her wardrobe!

One reason dark colors have this effect is that they draw the eye away from your body to your head, hands and feet, making you appear taller and slimmer. They also help to hide any bumps or bulges. By contrast, lighter colors emphasize your contours, as they are more likely to produce shadows in light-colored clothing.

Actually, though, if you want a slimming effect, an even more effective method is to wear the same solid color from top to toe. The single color creates an illusion of length, and prevents your body looking as if it has been divided in two at the waist.

Another tip if you want to look thin is to avoid wearing clothes with horizontal stripes, as these draw attention to your girth and make you look fatter. On the other hand, clothes with vertical stripes draw the eye upward, again making you look taller and slimmer (one reason pin-stripe suits are perennially popular among businessmen).

Why do birds fly in a V formation?

Scientists believe birds fly this way for two reasons. The first is that the V shape of the formation reduces the drag each bird experiences compared with flying alone. This is a result of the small updraft created by each bird for the bird flying behind it.

A bird in an updraft gains free lift, so it does not need to flap its wings as hard or as often. As a result, it does not tire as quickly and is able to fly further. According to one estimate, a flock of 25 birds in formation can fly up to 70% further than a solo bird using the same amount of energy.

Even though the V formation benefits all the birds, the one in front has to work the hardest. When this bird tires, it will drop out of the lead and fall back into one of the lines of the V. Another bird from further back will move forward to take the lead and maintain the formation. Much the same happens in team cycling races, where the lead cyclist has to work harder than those behind him, so the position is regularly rotated among other members of the team.

The other reason birds fly in a V is simply that it allows them to see one another more easily. This helps keep the flock together, and minimizes the possibility of losing some birds along the way as the formation crosses vast distances during migration.

09 Why do you shrink as you get older?

It's true that older people become a bit shorter over time. Shrinking takes place over a period of years, and may add up to only an inch or so off a person's adult height. This process can't be reversed, although it can be slowed or stopped. But why does it happen at all?

Part of the explanation comes down to gravity. Because for much of our lives we are standing up, the disks in our spine get compressed. They end up pressing closer together, which makes a person lose a little height and become shorter.

Another reason some older people shrink is a bone condition called osteoporosis. This occurs when bone is broken down and not enough new bone is made to replace it. Bones become smaller and weaker, and can easily break if someone with osteoporosis is injured. As years go by, a person with osteoporosis can get small bone breaks that are called compression fractures. These breaks cause collapse of the disks, meaning that over time a person with osteoporosis can become hunched or stooped.

As a matter of interest, everyone is a little shorter at the end of the day than they were at the beginning. That's because, as the day goes on, the disks of your spine gets compressed due to gravity, making you just a tiny bit shorter. Don't worry, though. Once you get a good night's rest, your body recovers, and in the morning, you're standing tall again.

10 Why does the moon appear bigger on the horizon than high in the sky?

This is actually an optical illusion. The reason it occurs is because our brain interprets objects on the horizon as being further away than those directly above us. Because the moon on the horizon seems further away than when it is directly overhead, our brain assumes it must be larger to compensate for its greater distance.

The same thing happens with the sun and other large, distant objects viewed low in the sky or near the horizon – mountains and tall buildings, for example. They may appear absolutely huge from a distance, but much less so as we get closer to them.

11 Why are tears salty?

In fact, it's not just tears – all the fluids in your body are at least a bit salty. All have some salts in them, and always some of the commonest salt, sodium chloride (the one that tastes the saltiest).

Your blood contains a little less than one per cent sodium chloride and your tears probably contain almost that much. Just for comparison, seawater contains about three per cent sodium chloride.

Salt performs a vital role in the human body, helping to transmit electrochemical messages, and to preserve the correct water balance, so we don't blow up like a balloon or shrivel like a raisin! So it's hardly surprising it turns up in all our body fluids too.

12 What causes an ice-cream headache?

An ice-cream headache is a sudden, stabbing headache that can occur just after eating or drinking something very cold. It's sometimes described as brain-freeze.

Ice-cream headaches are caused by a sudden cooling of the temperature in the roof of the mouth. The body senses this and reacts by trying to heat up the brain to 'protect' it from the cold. It does this by dilating the blood vessels in the brain, boosting the blood supply. This dilation is sensed by nearby pain receptors, which then send signals back to the brain via the trigeminal nerve, one of the main nerves serving the facial area. This nerve also senses facial pain, so the brain interprets the pain as coming from the forehead. The result can be sudden, excruciating pain, though it normally only lasts for around 20 to 60 seconds.

It's estimated that around 30 per cent of the population suffers from ice-cream headaches. If that includes you, the best way to avoid them is to keep any chilled foods or drinks on the side of your mouth and away from the top. Or have a cup of coffee instead.

13 Why does cling film cling?

Cling film, also called Saran Wrap, is widely used in catering for covering bowls, dishes, trays of sandwiches, and so on.

Cling film is made either from PVC or low density polyethylene that's treated to make it stretch. When you unroll the cling film, some of the electrons on the surface of one layer get pulled away onto the adjacent layer. This creates patches of positive and negative electrostatic charge.

Because cling film is a good insulator, this charge remains for quite a while. When you wrap the cling film around itself or another insulator (like glass), the electrostatic charge induces an opposite charge in the other surface. Because opposites attract, the two pieces stick together.

If you try using cling film on a conductor, such as a metal pan, it won't stick, because the electrical charge is immediately dispersed. Likewise, if you get cling film wet it won't work as well, because the water conducts the electricity away.

Cling film is an amazingly useful substance, but it's best not to leave it in direct contact with food for too long, as chemicals from the plastic can escape into the food. This applies especially with fatty foods. But for covering bowls and dishes to keep the contents safe, it's brilliant.

14 Why does helium make your voice go higher?

We've all done it. You go to a party and after a bit too much lemonade, those helium balloons become too much to resist. So what causes that hilarious squeaking? It helps if, to start with, you understand how our voices work.

When you talk, you force air over your vocal cords (flaps of tissue at the back of your throat), making them vibrate. This vibration produces a series of compression waves in the air, which a listener's ears interpret as sound.

Helium is less dense than the air we normally breathe, and that means sound waves travel through it faster than usual. When a series of compression waves (your voice) leaves the helium in your lungs and hits the denser air outside, the wave train is suddenly slowed down. The wave in front is slowed first, while the wave behind is still moving fast. Then the second wave is slowed while the third is still moving fast, and so on. It's like fast-moving traffic suddenly coming to a jam – all the cars bunch up close together.

Your ear interprets closely bunched sound waves as a higher pitch than widely spaced waves. So when your voice originates in helium and travels through the air to someone's ear, it sounds higher. If both you and the listener were in a room filled with helium, your voice would reach their ears faster than normal, but there would be no pitch change. Donald Duck would be amazed.

15 Why do bruises change color?

B ruises are caused when blood leaks out of blood vessels, typically as a result of a blow or fall, and is trapped under the skin. The different colors have to do with changes in the blood as it's broken down and reabsorbed.

Initially, bruises appear as red marks, red being (of course) the color of fresh blood. They then turn blue or dark purple within a few hours, then yellow or green as the bruise heals.

Different components of the blood have different colors, and these in turn lend color to the bruise. There are two major breakdown products that give bruises their distinctive colors. These are a green pigment called biliverdin and a yellow-brown pigment called bilirubin. Bruises usually start out as a dark blue or crimson; fade to violet, green, and dark yellow; then turn a pale yellow; and finally disappear completely. Minor bruises can hurt for a day or two, but they are normally harmless. Often, by the time the bruise has finally gone, the underlying tissue damage will have been long repaired.

If you are unlucky enough to have an accident, the best way to limit the amount of bruising you suffer is to apply a cold compress as soon as possible. This reduces the blood flow to the area, and hence the size of the bruise that develops.

16 Why can only some people waggle one eyebrow?

Like the ability to wiggle your ears, the ability to waggle one eyebrow is inherited. An estimated 20 per cent of people are born with this skill. Even if you aren't lucky enough to inherit this valuable talent from your parents, you may still be able to learn it.

One recommended method is to sit in front of a mirror and frown. This will pull both your eyebrows down. Then push up one eyebrow with a finger. See how this looks in the mirror, then try to hold the brow in position when you remove your finger. With practice, you should be able to hold the brow in its elevated position for a few seconds. From there, it is just a small step to learning to waggle your eyebrow unaided.

An interesting fact is that many people find it easier to waggle one eyebrow than the other. If you're trying to teach yourself the skill, therefore, it's a good idea to try both eyebrows, left and right, to see which feels more natural for waggling.

Finally, more men are born with the ability to waggle one eyebrow than women. At last, something men are naturally good at.

17 How does fabric conditioner make clothes soft?

Fabric conditioner, also called fabric softener, is a product added to laundry to make clothes feel softer. Depending on the brand, it can be added at the beginning of the wash cycle or during the rinse cycle. It can also come in sheets to be placed in the dryer.

Fabric conditioners coat the surface of clothing fibers with a thin layer of chemicals. This works in two ways. First, the chemicals have lubricant properties, which make the fibers feel smoother to the touch. And second, they are electrically conductive, preventing a build-up of static electricity in the clothes.

The latter is important, as static electricity can build up in fabrics during the washing and drying cycle. The static charge makes clothes stick together, making it more likely they will go into wrinkles, and it can even give you a brief electric shock. Adding fabric conditioner helps avoid this problem.

One potential disadvantage of using a fabric conditioner is that it reduces the ability of fabrics to absorb water, so it's best not to use one when washing towels. If towels are regularly washed using fabric conditioner, as the chemicals build up on them they will become stiff and unabsorbent.

18 Why do sodas go flat when they're warm?

The substance that gives soda its fizz is carbon dioxide gas. More carbon dioxide can be dissolved in a cold liquid than a warm one, so if you let your soda warm up, the carbon dioxide will escape faster. Eventually all of the gas will escape, leaving you with a flat soda.

The same thing will happen if you keep an open soda in the fridge; it'll just go flat a bit slower. With an unopened soda bottle, the pressure of carbon dioxide in the neck of the bottle stops any more gas escaping. But once you open the bottle you release this pressure, and the dissolved carbon dioxide can then start escaping into the atmosphere.

It follows that, as well as keeping your soda cool, you should try to avoid opening and closing the bottle too many times. Every time you open the bottle, the pressure is released and more gas can escape. When you put the cap back on, the pressure inside the bottle builds up again until no more gas can escape – but if you do this a few times, there will soon be no gas left dissolved. Result: a flat, horrible-tasting liquid, only fit for pouring down the drain.

19 Why does hair turn gray?

Hair gets its color from a substance called melanin. Melanin is produced by pigment cells, which are found at the root of every hair, in the hair follicle.

Melanin is the same chemical that makes our skin darker when we tan. The dark or light color of someone's hair depends on how much melanin each hair contains.

As we get older, the pigment cells in our hair follicles gradually die. When there are fewer pigment cells in a hair follicle, that strand of hair will no longer contain as much melanin and will be a more transparent color – gray, silver, or white – as it grows. As people continue to age, fewer pigment cells will be around to produce melanin. Eventually, the hair will look completely gray.

People can go gray at any age. It happens to some people when they are young – perhaps even in high school or college – whereas others may be in their thirties or forties before they see that first gray hair. How early it happens is determined by our genes. This means that most of us will start having gray hairs at around the same age our parents or grandparents first did.

We've all heard stories about a big shock or trauma turning someone gray overnight, but scientists don't really believe this happens. Even so, it doesn't stop many parents blaming their children for their gray hairs.

20 Why don't penguins' feet freeze?

This is an interesting question. In fact, penguins have an elaborate mechanism that stops their feet from freezing. It has two components.

First of all, penguins can control the rate of blood flowing to their feet by changing the diameter of the arteries that supply blood to them. In cold conditions this flow is reduced, while in warm the flow increases. Human beings can do this to a limited extent too, which is why our skin looks red when we are hot but pale if we are cold.

The other component is even more sophisticated. It takes the form of 'counter current heat exchangers' in the penguin's legs.

Warm blood and oxygen are supplied to the penguin's feet (and the rest of its body) via arteries. In the legs these break up into many small vessels that are closely entwined with similar numbers of venous vessels bringing cold blood back from the feet.

So, when heat is lost from the arterial vessels, the venous vessels running in the opposite direction pick it up and carry it back through the body, rather than out through the feet. This means that even in remote regions such as the feet, cells get oxygen but not much heat is lost through the skin.

All of this means that penguins are able to keep their feet at a constant temperature of about 2 °C – warm enough to avoid frostbite, but cold enough to avoid losing too much heat from the rest of their body.

21 Why do ears pop in planes?

Inside your ears, on the other side of your eardrums, are small, air-filled chambers. These chambers are connected to the back of your throat by the Eustachian tubes, two narrow channels that allow air in and out.

When a plane takes off, cabin air pressure decreases, but the pressure inside your ear lags behind. Your body therefore tries to equalize the pressure by allowing some air from your inner ear to escape through the Eustachian tubes. When they open, you feel the pressure release and hear the change because it's happening in your ear. This equalization of pressure produces the pop. The same thing happens in reverse when the plane comes down and cabin pressure increases.

22 Why does superglue not stick to the inside of its tube?

Superglue contains a chemical called cyanoacrylate. This reacts with water in the air to harden.

When superglue is manufactured, no moisture is allowed to enter the tube, so the glue doesn't harden. As soon as it is exposed to the air, however, it reacts with any moisture and solidifies.

If you want superglue to harden faster, try breathing on it, as the moisture in your breath promotes the hardening process. It's also why superglue sticks to your hands so well, as there's a plentiful supply of water on your skin.

It's a common complaint – an hour after a Chinese meal, you're hungry enough to eat another one.

And no, it's not a secret ingredient added by takeway owners to try to boost trade! Most experts now believe that this phenomenon is caused by the large amount of processed carbohydrates in many Chinese dishes. That includes rice, noodles, pancakes, prawn crackers, and so on.

These processed carbohydrates are quickly converted by the body into sugar and absorbed into the bloodstream. The raised blood sugar causes the body to produce a large burst of insulin, a hormone which takes sugar out of the blood and causes it to be stored in the liver and muscles.

The large burst of insulin released as a result of all the processed carbohydrates in our meal causes our blood sugar levels to plummet, and from a situation of very high blood sugar we suddenly go to a very low level. The body associates low blood sugar with hunger, and therefore sends the brain a signal we are hungry – even though at that moment the last thing we need is more food!

All this means that if you're on a diet, you should be careful about eating Chinese food, as it's very easy to overeat. And people with diabetes, whose bodies do not produce enough insulin, need to take extra care. For most healthy people, however, the occasional Chinese meal should not cause any real harm.

24 Why are yawns contagious?

We've all seen it – first one person in a group yawns, then another, and soon everyone in the room is doing it. Yawning really does seem to be contagious. But what is the reason?

In fact, nobody knows for sure. One theory is that, far from being a sign that we're ready to sleep, the purpose of yawning is to cool the brain so it operates more efficiently and keeps us awake. If we see someone yawning, therefore, we take it as a sign that we need to be more alert, so we yawn as a way of waking ourselves up.

Another recent psychological study found there was a close link between contagious yawning and empathy. In other words, people who were more prone to contagious yawning were better at judging other people's feelings and emotions. According to this research, contagious yawning is a way we communicate our understanding of the people around us and strengthen our emotional bonds with them. Ahh!

In fact, only around half of all people are susceptible to contagious yawning – but if that includes you, you can at least point out that it proves you are a more sensitive, sympathetic soul than your friends who are immune to it.

25 Why is it bad for your eyes to stare at an eclipse?

Solar eclipses – where the moon passes in front of the sun – are fascinating to observe, but to avoid damaging your eyes you should never stare at one directly. There are several good reasons for this.

First, even if only a thin sliver of sunlight is visible, this is still bright enough to burn out the retina at the back of your eye if you stare directly at it, leaving your vision permanently damaged.

In addition, at the moment of eclipse everything goes dark and hence the pupils in our eyes expand to help us see better. But as soon as the moon moves on, a sudden burst of sunlight occurs. If our pupils are still expanded, this burst of light can cause a lot more harm.

And, of course, during an eclipse, our curiosity makes us want to stare at the sun for longer then the usual fraction of a second. This makes it much more likely we will damage our eyes.

If you want to look at an eclipse, the best advice is to use special 'eclipse glasses' that filter out most of the sunlight. You can also project the image of the eclipse onto the ground using a pinhole projector. Just punch a hole in a piece of paper and hold it a few feet above a smooth, light-colored surface. A small image of the eclipse should then appear, which is safe to view.

26 What is at the center of a black hole?

A black hole is an area of extremely dense matter resulting from the collapse of a star. It has a very high gravitational field, which (according to Einstein's General Theory of Relativity) distorts time and space around it.

Black holes are so-called because nothing, including light, can escape from them. Despite this, the presence of black holes can be deduced by scientists by the way their powerful gravitational fields affect the stars and other objects surrounding them.

Around a black hole there is an undetectable surface which marks the point of no return, called an event horizon. Once an object has entered the event horizon, there is no way out. Anything drawn into the black hole ultimately becomes part of its ultra-dense core.

Most scientists believe that at the center of a black hole is something called a singularity. This is defined as a point of infinite density and zero volume. Nobody really knows what would happen here, as in essence nature divides our equations by zero. As you may have learned in mathematics lessons, you cannot divide anything by zero and get a sensible answer.

Some scientists believe that with certain types of black hole, it might be possible for a spaceship (say) to enter the event horizon and, rather than being absorbed, come out somewhere else in the universe. This is the 'wormhole' so beloved of science-fiction writers. If this proves right, one day human beings really could 'go where no man has gone before'!

You may have heard that cows are the biggest contributors to air pollution through the amount of methane gas they produce – but is that really true?

It is certainly the case that cows emit methane, mostly from belching, but also from flatulence. And their feces emit even more once they start to rot. Methane is one of the so-called greenhouse gases which cause global warming – it is 21 times worse in this respect than carbon dioxide, the gas that normally gets most of the blame.

As there are so many cows in the world, there is no doubt the methane they produce contributes significantly to air pollution and global warming. Because it is difficult to measure, it is impossible to say for sure whether cows are worse polluters than motor vehicles, the other main offenders. In addition, motor vehicles produce a range of other gases, some of which are potentially even more damaging to the environment than methane (e.g. ozone).

Even so, cows are unquestionably big polluters, so a lot of work is currently going on to find foods they can be fed that will produce less gas when they are digested. Some farms also have systems for capturing the methane their cows produce and recycling it as fuel.

28 Why don't you remember being a baby?

If you think back to your earliest memory, it's probably no further back than when you were about three. In fact, you can probably come up with only a few memories from between the ages of three and seven, though family photo albums may trigger a few more. Psychologists refer to this inability of most adults to remember events from early life, including their birth, as childhood amnesia.

Nobody is exactly sure why it occurs. One reason, however, is likely to be that when we are very young our brains are still developing. Babies can remember things, but their memories for events don't last longer than 24 hours. This is probably because the brain structures involved in making memories for events aren't mature yet.

As we get older, other factors also come into play. For example, storing specific memories is difficult unless you have a context in which to place them ('holidays', for example). For their first few years, children don't have this framework – they need to build it up from their experiences.

Finally, the older you are, the more things you will have seen and done, and therefore stored in your memory. Storing new memories has a slight impact on your ability to remember older ones. As a result, the older an experience, the harder it is to remember all the details. Since babyhood is as far back as it goes, those memories are the hardest to retrieve.

Having your foot 'fall asleep' is an odd sensation. Many people say it's due to cutting off the circulation to your foot, but that isn't strictly true. It's mainly caused by communication between your foot and brain being disrupted.

The situation normally occurs when you've been putting pressure on your foot for a while, maybe by sitting or lying on it. When you do this, the nerves in and around the foot get squashed, which stops them transmitting messages properly. In addition, the blood supply to your foot may be restricted, which starves the nerve cells in the area of oxygen and can cause them to behave abnormally.

The result of this is that you lose some of the feeling in your foot, and – because it works both ways – your brain also has trouble telling your foot what to do.

After you stand up and the nerves are no longer compressed, the feeling in your foot soon comes back. It might feel a bit tingly as this happens, like pins and needles. But this only lasts a few seconds, and won't harm you. If you don't want it to happen again, though, don't sit on your feet or put them in other positions where you're squashing the nerves.

30 Why is a golf ball not smooth?

The reason modern golf balls have dimples is not just for their looks. Golf was originally played with smooth balls, but in the early 20th century some keen players discovered that their older, scratched balls actually traveled further, to the surprise of many at the time.

As experts began to look into this phenomenon, they discovered that all those scratches were functioning as turbulators. Essentially, a turbulator is something that increases the amount of turbulence created by an object.

In the case of the well-worn golf ball, the uneven surface was introducing turbulence into the layer of air around the ball as it sailed towards its target. The presence of turbulence reduces the drag on the ball, which allows it to travel further.

Typical modern golf balls have 300–400 dimples, and are capable of traveling up to four times the distance achievable with the original smooth balls. Part of this improvement is that, along with the fact that golf balls have dimples today, they are also sealed with a laminate. The combination helps keep drag to a minimum, making it easier to control both the distance and the direction the ball travels.

The design of the dimples is still being refined and improved, and no doubt future golf balls will travel even longer distances. Fore!

31 What are liver spots?

Liver spots are blemishes on the skin associated with ageing and exposure to ultraviolet radiation from the sun.

They range in color from light brown to red or black, and are located in areas most often exposed to the sun, particularly the hands, face, shoulders, arms, and forehead, and the head if bald. The spots are oval or irregularly shaped, different sizes and always have sharply defined borders.

Liver spots are not related to the liver physiologically. They got their name from an incorrect belief that they were caused by liver problems, and also because their color is similar to that of raw liver.

Liver spots get their color from melanin, the same pigment that gives our skin and hair its color. Melanin is produced by the skin to help protect itself from sunlight. From the age of 40 onwards the skin is less able to regenerate from sun exposure, and liver spots are very common in this age group, particularly in those who spend a lot of time in the sunshine.

The good news is that in the vast majority of cases liver spots pose no threat, and no medical treatment is required.

32 Why do cookies go soft but cake turns hard?

It's all down to their water content. Biscuits have less water in them than the air around them, so they absorb water from the air and go soft.

Cakes are normally moist and contain more water, so it evaporates into the atmosphere, causing the cake to go hard.

A lot depends on the amount of water in the atmosphere, though. Cookies do not go soft in the desert, no matter how long they are left out, because there is no moisture in the air for them to absorb.

33 Why do clouds get dark before it rains?

It is the thickness, or depth, of clouds that makes them look gray.

Clouds are made of tiny droplets of water or ice. These droplets scatter all colors of light equally. When light contains all colors, we perceive it as white.

When clouds are thin, they let most of the light through and appear white. But the thicker they get, the less light makes it through. As their thickness increases, the bottoms of clouds look darker, but still scatter all colors. We see this as gray. The thicker the clouds become, the grayer they look, and the more likely they are to rain on us.

34 Why does spicy food make your nose run?

Many people notice that after eating a meal of hot, spicy foods, their nose begins to run.

There is one very simple reason for this. Spicy foods contain a substance called capsaicin, which is found in hot peppers.

Capsaicin is an irritant, and as the mucus membranes in the nose are exposed to it, they become inflamed and increase mucus production. Capsaicin also causes the blood vessels in the face to dilate, meaning that someone eating a hot curry may also get a red face and start sweating.

The capsaicin in spicy food is highly unlikely to cause you any permanent harm. Indeed, it can act as a nasal decongestant, helping loosen up excess mucus in the nose and throat. However, experts do not recommend that people suffering from colds eat spicy foods. Although the decongestant effect might provide some short-term relief, eating spicy foods also triggers more mucus production.

If you eat a hot curry while you are congested, you are likely to end up even more bunged up and miserable than when you started, even if you enjoy some temporary relief while eating it. Better stick to the chicken soup after all.

35 Why does a black car heat faster than a white one?

There's a simple answer to this. Black paint absorbs light from the sun and turns it into heat, whereas white tends to reflect it back into the atmosphere. For the same reason, if it's a hot day, we normally wear light-colored clothes for going out.

In fact, the reason any surface appears dark is because it's absorbing more energy than a light-colored one. Less light is bouncing off it and available to scatter towards your eye. The color of an object indicates the wavelength of light being reflected by that object (or the color of light not being absorbed). An object that appears black is absorbing all colors of light, while one that appears white is reflecting them all.

The American popular science TV show MythBusters actually tested this principle in an episode aired in January 2003. They used two identical cars, one black and the other white, and left them out in the summer heat with thermometers in both. By mid-afternoon the black car had heated up to a temperature of 135°F, while the white car topped off at 126°F, almost 10 degrees cooler. In Celsius the black car was 57°C and the white was 52°, so a five-degree difference.

If you want to stay cool in your car, therefore, getting a white one is the way to go. Or buy a model with air conditioning.

36 Why do you see stars when you're hit on the head?

We've all seen cartoons where a character gets hit on the head, and stars appear and float in a circle above them. It can happen in real life as well, but it's definitely not as funny as when it happens in a cartoon.

Seeing stars typically happens when you are struck on the back of your head. This is where the brain's occipital lobes, which control vision, are located. The sudden impact causes the nerve cells in this part of the brain to misfire, and we interpret this as twinkling stars.

Other things as well as a blow on the head can cause this to happen, for instance a lack of blood reaching the brain, and thus a lack of oxygen. Most often, this happens after standing up quickly, or straightening up after bending over. It can also happen if you're dehydrated, perhaps after running a marathon or some other vigorous form of exercise.

If you see stars, it doesn't necessarily mean you've suffered a serious injury, but it's certainly a sign that you should sit down and take it easy for a while. It's also a good idea to get some fluids inside you, in case dehydration is playing a part. If it happens regularly you should see a doctor, as this can be a sign of low blood pressure or some other medical condition.

This typically occurs when the muscles in the neck get chilled and contract. If this happens over several hours, the muscles seize up and can't easily relax again, resulting in the misery of a stiff neck that can stay with you the whole day.

To avoid a stiff neck, it's best to avoid sleeping right next to an open window or – for that matter – a fan or air-conditioning unit. Of course, having a window open in your bedroom to let in some fresh air is a healthy thing – what you need to avoid is cold drafts.

If, nevertheless, you do wake up with a stiff neck, treatment involves unclenching the muscles there. Gently massaging the neck should help – either do this yourself or (even better) get a friend to do it for you. Another good tactic is applying gentle warmth to the area, perhaps by means of a hot-water bottle. Popular anti-inflammatory drugs can reduce the pain and make it easier for the muscles in your neck to relax again.

We've all seen comic strips where a child is accidentally lifted off his feet by a bunch of helium balloons. But is this possible – and how many balloons would it require?

The American popular science TV show MythBusters tested this out in an episode originally aired in November 2004. They found that it could be done, but it took a very large number of balloons. The team discovered that it took 3,500 ordinary party balloons to lift an average four-year-old girl of around 40 lbs/18 kg just a few feet off the ground.

A more scientific approach is to calculate the amount of lift in each balloon. A standard party balloon one foot/30 cm in diameter has a capacity of around 14 liters. Helium has a lifting force of 1 gram per liter, so a standard balloon would have a lifting force of 14 gm.

A 40 lb child is around 18 kg, so dividing this by 14 gm gives a figure of around 1,300 balloons to lift them off the ground. That's a lot less than the MythBusters' figure, but of course this theoretical calculation doesn't allow for the weight of the balloons themselves or the string needed to attach them.

Either way, if you buy a bunch of helium balloons and hold them by the string, you may be pleased or disappointed to learn that there is absolutely no risk of floating away and ending up in South America.

39 Why does your tongue stick if you lick a cold metal pole?

The short answer to this is that the saliva on your tongue freezes between the skin of your tongue and the cold metal. The frozen saliva then forms a glue-like bond between the two surfaces.

For this to happen, the temperature of the metal must be below 0°C/32°F, otherwise the water cannot freeze. The lower the temperature of the metal, the quicker your tongue will stick to it. Even your hand may stick to a cold metal pole if it is a little sweaty – for example, if you have just taken it out of a warm glove.

This works better with metal objects than, say, plastic or wood, because metal conducts the heat away faster. That means the heat has gone from your tongue before your body has a chance to replenish it, so your saliva freezes more quickly.

If you ever find yourself in this embarrassing situation, don't jerk your tongue away, or you could leave a layer of skin from your tongue on the pole. Pouring warm water over it will melt the ice and break the bond. However, wouldn't it really be better not to go licking cold metal poles in the first place?

We can only see as far as the horizon because of the curvature of the earth. At the horizon, the land (or sea) curves below our line of vision.

How far the horizon appears depends on a number of things, including our height and where we are standing. An adult standing with eyes about 5.5 ft/1.7 m from the ground will see the horizon at a distance of 2.9 miles/4.6 km.

However, this rule applies only if you are looking across perfectly flat ground, or out to sea while standing at sea level. From higher up you can see much further. If you stood at the top of Mount Everest, for example (which is 29,029 feet or 8,848 meters tall), the horizon would be about 230 miles/370 km away.

In addition, we need to take into account the effect of refraction, which bends rays of light as they pass through the atmosphere. This makes the horizon even further away. Cold weather increases the amount of atmospheric refraction, so in a particularly chilly location such as Antarctica, people have been able to see for hundreds of miles.

But just as weather can assist our view, it can also hinder it. Mist and fog often limit visibility to below what you could expect based on height. And, of course, even the best viewing conditions aren't much good if there's a mountain in your way.

41 Where does the salt in the sea come from?

The salt in the sea comes originally from the land. Rivers carry dissolved salts from the rocks they flow over into the oceans.

Volcanic eruptions also contribute. Much of the ash and dust they release settles into the oceans, where some dissolves, adding to the salt content.

The oceans usually contain 35 parts of salt for every 1,000 parts of seawater. This is lower in some places where there is a lot of fresh water coming in. It is higher where the sun is very strong and evaporates more of the water. An example is the Dead Sea, between Israel and Jordan, which has ten times the salt content of other seawater. This allows anyone to easily float on the Dead Sea because of its greater density.

It is unlikely that the oceans will become any saltier. In fact, the sea has had about the same amount of salt in it for hundreds of millions of years. The salt content has reached a steady state. Dissolved salts are being removed from seawater to form new minerals at the bottom of the ocean as fast as rivers and other sources are introducing new salt.

42 Why do old ladies grow beards?

It's largely down to hormonal changes. As women age, their estrogen (female hormone) level declines. This disrupts the delicate balance with the male hormone testosterone.

Testosterone is produced naturally in women's bodies (though not nearly as much as in men, who produce ten times as much). It has many beneficial effects for women, including promoting bone growth, sharpening mental faculties, and assisting the growth of thick, lustrous hair. Estrogen and testosterone act together to produce a normal hormonal balance in women.

As women get older, however, and their estrogen levels fall, the male hormone can become dominant. As a result, old ladies often experience changes to their body which are more typically associated with men. As well as growing beards and other body hair, other side-effects can include a deepening of the voice, baldness, acne, and so on.

There is also a genetic factor. If your mother and grandmother developed facial hair as they got older, it's very likely that you will too.

So if Grandma kisses you and it tickles a bit, don't worry, it's perfectly natural. Just resist the urge to buy her a shaver for Christmas.

43 What makes waves curl as they reach the shore?

It's all down to friction. As the water gets shallower, its forward movement is slowed by friction against the sea floor. This has the effect of slowing the waves down and pushing them together.

That makes each wave steeper, especially on its front side. As the water gets shallower, the waves get steeper and steeper, until they fall over and break.

Usually a wave breaks when the water depth is about one and a third times the height of the wave. If a wave is 1 m or 3.3 feet high, for example, it will start to break when the water is about 1.3 m/4.5 ft deep.

44 Why does a house creak more at night?

Most houses get cooler at night, as outside temperatures fall and the heating is turned off (or at least down) while we sleep.

Most things contract when they get cooler, so as temperatures drop, the wooden boards and metal parts that make up the house shrink a little.

The metal parts contract more than the wood, so the nails, pipes, air ducts, and so on rub against the wood. Wood also rubs against wood. All that rubbing can make creaking sounds. And, of course, at night, when the house is quiet, we are more likely to notice them. Okay, you *might* have ghosts as well, but this natural explanation is a lot more probable.

45 Why do knuckles crack?

Some people – not all – can crack their knuckles by moving them rapidly in a certain way.

One popular method is to clench your hands so they interlock, then suddenly straighten your fingers and push slightly into each knuckle. That push should generate an immediate crack.

Knuckle-cracking is believed to be caused by a sudden reduction in the pressure in the fluid that surrounds your knuckle joints. When you stretch or bend your fingers, you're causing the bones of the knuckle joint to pull apart. As they do, the capsule of fluid that surrounds the joint is stretched, so increasing its volume. With this increase in volume comes a decrease in pressure. As the pressure of the joint fluid drops, gases dissolved in it become less soluble, forming bubbles through a process called cavitation. When the joint is stretched far enough, the pressure in the capsule drops so low that these bubbles burst, producing the pop we associate with knuckle-cracking.

It takes about twenty minutes for the gas released in popping to be reabsorbed into the joint fluid. During this time, your knuckles won't crack. Once the gas is redissolved, cavitation is again possible, and you can start popping your joints again.

As long as you don't do it excessively, cracking your knuckles is a harmless pastime.

It's true – drinking a glass of warm milk before you go to bed really can help you get a good night's rest.

The main reason is that milk contains a plentiful supply of the amino acid tryptophan. Once tryptophan reaches your brain, it boosts the production of serotonin, a neuro-transmitter that helps you sleep.

Because carbohydrates also increase serotonin production – which is why you may feel sleepy after a big plate of pasta – the carbs in milk will also help you to drift off.

And another benefit of drinking milk at night is that it contains calcium. Calcium helps the body absorb tryptophan faster, thus ensuring that its sleep-inducing properties kick in sooner.

Whether the milk is warm or cold makes no difference to the level of tryptophan or how quickly it reaches your brain. However, the warmth of the milk can provide a feeling of comfort, whereas cold drinks may deliver a jolt to your system – good for waking you up in the morning, not so good last thing at night!

There is no difference in the levels of tryptophan in skimmed or whole fat milk, so to be extra-healthy, always use skimmed milk for your bedtime drink.

Up until quite recently – around 100 years ago – there were no communication aids like radio or telephones, and no mass media seen by everyone, like films or TV. No-one traveled much unless they really had to, and as a result language evolved quite differently in different places.

In the same country, people from one village, town or tribe could quite easily live their whole lives and never visit the next town. As a result, many different accents developed, along with differences in vocabulary, slang, and so on. Another factor in countries such as the US was the arrival of waves of settlers from different countries, each with their own native language which became incorporated into the local dialect.

It's only in the last century – a very short time in historical terms – that all this has changed. People nowadays travel around a lot more in search of work, and almost everyone has access to television and other media in which a wide range of accents can be heard.

As a result of all this, differences in accents are fading gradually, though it is likely to be many years yet before we all sound alike.

48 Why do male mammals have nipples?

Nearly all male mammals possess nipples, with a few exceptions, which include rats and horses.

The most widely-accepted explanation for this is that in most mammals (including human beings) nipples develop in the embryo before it has differentiated into a male or a female.

In the case of human beings, boys are born not only with nipples but also with mammary glands which can produce milk. However, these only develop into breasts in the female, as a result of the female hormones estrogen and progesterone, which are produced in large quantities in females at the onset of puberty.

In men, the nipples do not perform any useful function. They are simply there because they are needed by the female. Because their presence does not appear to disadvantage men in any other way, there has not been any particular evolutionary pressure to lose them.

One thing that has worried scientists recently is that the increasing pollution in food, water and the air may be causing males of all species to take on female characteristics, as some of it is converted in the body into estrogen. In theory this could result in human males growing breasts. When therapists suggest that men get in touch with their feminine side, this is probably not what they have in mind.

49 Why does peeling onions make you cry?

Who hasn't peeled an onion and had to wipe away the tears from their eyes? Here's a simple explanation for why it happens.

Inside the onion cells there are chemical compounds that contain sulfur. When you cut into an onion its cells are broken, and those chemicals then undergo a reaction that transforms them into a sulfur-based gas, which is released into the air.

This gas reacts with the moisture in your eyes, forming sulfuric acid. This produces a burning sensation. The brain reacts by telling your tear ducts to produce more water, to dilute the irritating acid. So you cry to protect your eyes from the acid.

Another reflex to rid the eyes of a foreign substance, that of rubbing them with your hands, can actually make the situation worse. Because our hands are moist they also become coated with sulfuric acid, which we then rub directly into our eyes, irritating them further.

To avoid this problem, one method is to cut the onion under water. The gas released then dissolves in the water rather than escaping into the air. You can also put the onion in the freezer for ten minutes before you cut it. Cold temperatures slow down the rate at which gas is released, so less of it will reach your eyes.

The answer to this, perhaps surprisingly, is very little. Researchers at the University of Leeds (UK) recently calculated that around 1.5 million Titanic-sized icebergs each year are melting into the sea every year in the Arctic and Antarctic. This is causing sea level to rise by just 49 micrometers per year – literally, a hair's breadth.

At that rate it would take 200 years for the oceans to rise by 1 cm (less than half an inch) as a result of melting sea ice. If all the floating ice in the world melted, it would cause sea levels to rise by just 4 cm (1.6 in).

But don't breathe a sigh of relief just yet. Global warming is raising sea levels in another, much more significant way. As water gets warmer, it becomes less dense, and therefore takes up more space. As the overall temperature of the water increases, it expands, making the oceans rise.

In 1995, the Intergovernmental Panel on Climate Change issued a report which contained various projections of the sea level change by the year 2100. They estimated that the sea will rise around 50 cm/1.7 ft, with the lowest estimates at 15 cm/13 in and the highest at 95 cm/3.2 ft. The rise will come mainly from thermal expansion of the oceans. These are not trivial amounts – this level of change would have a dramatic effect on many coastal cities, especially during storms.

51 Why does cream whip?

When you whip cream, you are introducing air bubbles into it. As you continue whipping, proteins from the milk are trapped in the walls of the air bubbles, creating a structure that holds the cream in a sort of foam. Whipped cream is about double the volume of the original.

Milk has the same protein content as cream, yet you can beat milk until the cows come home (ho ho!) and still never achieve whipped milk. The reason is the lower fat content of milk. Milk does form protein air pockets just like whipped cream, but they burst almost as soon as you make them.

The higher fat content of cream (it must be at least 30% to be whippable) means it flows much more slowly, so the bubbles are slower to break down. In addition, the behavior of the fat aids in creating a foam structure. The fats gather in the bubble walls where the protein structure is forming. The fat molecules act like a sort of glue, helping to hold the protein molecules in place. In essence, you and your whisk are creating a fat and protein 'net' in which to catch air.

If you go on beating cream, the fat droplets will start sticking together, forming lumps. These are actually butter. The more you go on whipping, the bigger the butter lumps will become. Eventually, you will be left with butter and liquid buttermilk. Fine in their place, but not nearly as nice on your apple pie.

52 Why do you need less sleep when you're old?

As we get older as adults, we seem to need less sleep. One study published in *Sleep* magazine in February 2010 found that older adults slept about 20 minutes less per night than middle-aged adults, who in turn slept 23 minutes less than young adults.

Nobody is sure why we need less sleep when we're old, or indeed why we need sleep at all. One thing that's clear, however, is that if we don't get enough, our health and well-being can be badly affected. Lack of sleep reduces our ability to pay attention or remember new information. It also causes increased appetite, leading to a greater risk of obesity.

Other consequences of sleeplessness include a higher risk of diabetes and heart problems, as well as psychiatric conditions such as depression. Sleep appears to be necessary for our brains and bodies to function effectively, though scientists still aren't sure why.

One possible explanation for older adults needing less sleep is that they are more likely to take naps in the day. This means they don't then need as much sleep at night.

Children and teenagers need more sleep than adults. This is because their brains are still developing and they are learning lots of new things every day. Children aged between 5 and 12 need 10–11 hours per night, while teenagers from 13 to 17 need around 9 hours. This compares with 7–8 hours for most adults.

53 Why does a bee die after it stings but a wasp doesn't?

This basically happens because bees (most of them, anyway) have barbed stings that get stuck after stinging you.

Stings originally evolved to fight other insects. When a bee stings another insect it punches a hole in the insect's hard exterior skeleton and has no difficulty withdrawing the sting through the hole it has produced.

It's the bee's misfortune that mammals have a flexible skin. If a bee stings a mammal (such as a human being) the skin closes up around the sting and grips it. If it has penetrated far enough for the barbs to be trapped when the bee tries to withdraw, the sting is pulled out of the bee's abdomen, along with the venom sac, the muscles that pump the venom, and the nerve ganglion controlling the muscles. This is why a sting can continue to inject venom even after the bee has gone.

If a bee loses its sting it doesn't die immediately but within a matter of hours, because of the internal injuries caused by the sting being pulled out.

Wasps don't have barbed stings, so they can easily withdraw them, even after stinging a mammal. That means they don't die, and can go straight on and sting someone else if they like.

54 Can you really start a fire by rubbing two sticks together?

It can certainly be done, but you will need patience, a lot of effort, and a bit of luck!

Start by collecting a pile of tinder – dry materials that catch fire easily (paper, tree bark, dry pine needles etc.). Now take two sticks and rub them together as hard as you can near the tinder. The friction will create heat, and if you are lucky – and energetic enough – a spark will leap out and ignite the tinder. Once the tinder is burning, you can use it to light your fire.

Or you could just bring a box of matches of course!

55 Why does garlic make your breath smell?

Garlic contains many sulfurous compounds. When consumed, these compounds actually feed odor-causing (but otherwise harmless) bacteria in the mouth. The bacteria become more numerous as a result, and bad breath is the outcome.

Unfortunately there is no cure for garlic breath, apart from not eating garlic. That would be a shame, as many people enjoy the flavor, and it has many health benefits. Eating a sprig of fresh parsley with your meal is said to help. But perhaps the best solution is to ensure that all your friends like garlic as well. If you've all eaten garlic, you are much less likely to notice it on one another's breath.

56 Why do teeth chatter when you're cold?

Teeth chattering when we get cold is really just a form of localized shivering. Shivering is a method used by the body to generate heat when we get cold.

Our bodies usually maintain a constant temperature of 98.6 degrees Fahrenheit – that's the temperature at which the cells of the body work best. If there is any significant change from this, it's sensed by a part of the brain called the hypothalamus. When we get too cold, the hypothalamus alerts the rest of the body to begin warming us up.

Shivering is one method the body uses for this. When we shiver, our muscles expand and contract rapidly to produce extra body heat. When our muscles do this, they convert energy to heat, just as happens when we exercise.

Shivering is therefore our muscles working by themselves to heat us up. This is an attempt by the body to prevent a condition called hypothermia, where our temperature falls too low to survive and our body slowly shuts down.

If you find your teeth chattering, chances are you'll also experience other symptoms such as goose-flesh and shivering in all your muscles. It's nature's way of telling you it's definitely time to get back in the warm again.

57 Why do you have an appendix if it has no function?

The human appendix is a short, blind-ended tube found near the junction of the small intestine and the large intestine. In most people it is barely four inches/10 cm long.

The appendix does not appear to perform any important function in the body. This is demonstrated by the fact that we do not experience any ill effects, if for medical reasons, it has to be removed.

Most scientists believe the appendix is a remnant of an organ which has lost its original function. According to this theory, our early ancestors lived on a diet of leaves and bark, and a long intestine was required to digest this. As human beings evolved, our diet changed as well, and a long appendix was no longer needed. Some experts believe that in many generations the human appendix will vanish altogether.

Recently, however, some scientists have suggested that the appendix may indeed perform a useful role. The latest theory is that it stores friendly bacteria for help in digestion, and helps you recover these bacteria after an illness.

The appendix is, unfortunately, susceptible to infection, the results of which can be serious or even fatal. As a result, seven per cent of the general population will have their appendix removed at some point in their lives. But don't worry if that includes you – you can live very happily without it.

Scientists believe that the long time human beings take to reach adulthood is mainly down to the time it takes for our large and complex brains to develop fully. Compared with other mammals, humans have the largest brain size compared to overall body size.

Our brains are not fully formed at birth. They continue to develop through childhood and adolescence, and even into adulthood. Human beings can only afford their large brains thanks to the long period their parents look after them.

There is also a social aspect to this. Human beings simply take a long time to learn all the many skills they need to participate fully in society and bring up children themselves.

Incidentally, human beings aren't the only creatures to reach adulthood late. Most primates (e.g. chimps and monkeys) develop more slowly and have longer lifespans than other mammals. For instance, chimpanzees enter puberty at around the age of seven, and have their first offspring between the ages of 11 and 23.

So if you're young and your parents tell you off for doing something stupid, you can always reply that you couldn't help it, your brain isn't fully developed yet.

Why do bananas make other fruit ripen quicker?

Bananas release an odorless gas called ethylene that is vital to their ripening process. Ethylene also makes most other fruits ripen faster.

Ethylene gas is used in greenhouses to ripen fruits commercially. The gas is also used by companies that ship unripe fruits across the world and then expose them to ethylene to ripen the fruits before selling them.

You can make a bunch of bananas ripen more quickly by putting it in a plastic bag to trap the ethylene they release. You can also use this property of bananas to help ripen other fruits. Put hard avocados, pears or peaches in a bag with a banana for a day or two, and the gas released by the bananas will stimulate the other fruits to ripen.

On the other hand, if you don't want other fruits to ripen too quickly, it's best to store them away from bananas.

As a matter of interest, apples also give off a lot of ethylene as they ripen, and especially if they get over-ripe. This can quickly cause all the other apples kept with them to get over-ripe and rot as well. Hence the saying, one bad apple spoils the barrel.

This is one of those questions we've all wondered about. In one sense it's impossible to answer, as none of us will ever know what it's like to be inside somebody else's head.

However, it seems highly probable that most of us do see colors in the same way. There are two main reasons for this.

First, we all have the same light- and color-sensitive cells in the retinas of our eyes. When light of a particular wavelength falls on one of these cells, it transmits a message to the visual area of our brain, which we interpret as vision. As we all have the same basic 'wiring', it seems highly likely we all see colors in the same way.

Another strong indication is that if you shine a light of a specific wavelength, most people will give it the same name, for example, blue.

As you may know, some people (more men than women) suffer from color blindness. People with red/green color blindness, for example, are unable to see a difference between these two colors.

For many centuries color blindness didn't cause any real problems and people were unaware the condition even existed. In modern industrial societies, however, the inability to distinguish between a red light and a green light (say) can have serious consequences. Many jobs in the military, for example, are closed to people with color blindness.

To start with, it isn't correct to say that monkeys evolved into humans. In fact, both species evolved separately from a common ancestor, sometimes described as the missing link.

Even so, just because one species evolves from another, it doesn't necessarily mean the original species will become extinct. The older species will still survive as long as it continues to adapt to its environment. Evolution works more like branches off a tree than a ladder.

The question implies that human beings are in some way better than monkeys. In fact, the truth is that they are just adapted for different environments. A human being could not survive in the treetops of the Brazilian rainforest, any more than a rainforest monkey could get along in a city such as New York – each species has evolved to fit a specific ecological niche.

There are lots of species of plants and animals all existing at the same time because they all perform different roles on the planet. One species only replaces another when they are directly competing for the same limited resources. That's probably why there is only one species of human being – there wasn't enough room on our planet for two.

62 Why do people put steak on a black eye?

You've probably seen cartoons in which a raw steak is slapped onto the face of an injured character to help heal a black eye.

In fact, doing this is highly inadvisable. Raw meat typically has all sorts of harmful bacteria (such as *E. Coli*) on it. Putting this into contact with damaged skin is quite likely to lead to an infection.

What people who swear by steaks fail to realize is that what was actually helping the black eye was the cold. Typically, they grab a steak out of the freezer, then press it against their injured eye. In this case, the cold acts to bring the swelling down. But the steak itself does nothing, apart from possibly give you an infection.

If you are unlucky enough to suffer a black eye, the best thing to do is apply an ice pack for a few minutes to reduce the swelling, then take it easy for a while. Taking a mild anti-inflammatory medicine might not be a bad idea either. The wound will heal quickly. If you must use a steak, make sure it is frozen, and wrapped in a bag or some other material that can prevent your skin from actually making contact with the meat. And have the steak for your dinner later.

What are the bubbles that appear as water begins to boil?

The bubbles are water vapor, combined with a little air.

When water reaches 100°C/212°F it turns into a gas called water vapor, otherwise known as steam. This is less dense than the water around it, so it rises to the top, where it escapes into the air.

In addition, water contains a certain amount of dissolved air. The solubility of the gases in air (mainly nitrogen and oxygen) reduces as water gets hotter, so they also appear as bubbles. The bubbles that appear in water before it gets close to boiling are mainly dissolved air coming out of solution rather than water vapor.

Most of the bubbles in a kettle start at the bottom, because that's where the heat is. As the water approaches boiling point you will see larger bubbles of steam forming at the bottom and turning back into water as they rise to the cooler layer above. This process is what gives a kettle coming to the boil its distinctive 'bubbling' sound. Once water gets to 100°C/212°F it does not get any hotter. Instead, all the heat energy goes into converting the liquid water to steam.

Right, who wants a cup of tea, then?

64

More people are living today than ever before. Does that mean that the world is heavier with all the extra people?

It's quite true that there are more people living today than at any time in the past. However, that doesn't mean the world is any heavier as a result.

The weight of our planet is independent of the number of people on it. The main reason is that all the matter that makes up people comes from the earth. It doesn't matter if there are two people or twenty billion – the material that makes up their bodies comes from the earth, and eventually (when they die) it returns to it. And the whole time their weight, alive or dead, is part of the total weight of the planet.

In order to make the world heavier, we'd need to invite extra-terrestrials in large numbers. If we assume these aliens are a bit bigger than us at 220 lbs/100 kg each, we'd need about a trillion aliens to increase the weight of the world by 0.0016%. Of course they'd probably eat all the food and leave the place a wreck, but even then the change to the planet's total weight would be negligible!

As a matter of interest, while the total weight of everyone on earth is obviously no small sum, it is still tiny compared with the weight of the earth itself. It has been calculated that the mass of all the people on earth is about one-and-a-half trillionth the weight of the earth.

65 Why do people talk in their sleep?

Talking in your sleep is actually quite common, with five per cent of adults and up to 50 per cent of young children reported to do it. Of course, you'll only know if that includes you if somebody tells you!

Sleep talk usually occurs when we're dreaming. Normally while we're asleep our muscles are effectively paralyzed, to stop us damaging ourselves by acting out our dreams – but in particularly scary or exciting dreams, the muscles controlling speech may start to function again, causing us to speak out loud whatever we are saying in our dreams.

Talking in your sleep isn't usually anything to worry about. Although it may be a problem for your partner if you keep waking them up with your nocturnal mutterings!

66 Why do fingers and toes wrinkle in the bath?

When your fingers and toes get wrinkly, your skin is actually expanding, not wrinkling up. Your skin has several layers. The top layer is covered by a water-resistant oil called sebum. When you stay in the bath for a long time, especially if you're using soap and other lotions, this oil is washed away. Without it, your fingers are no longer waterproof, and water is able to get into the top layer of your skin. The extra water in your fingers causes the skin to swell and expand in some places, but not in others – making your digits look like prunes.

This is a controversial subject. We all know people who claim they can't sing because they are 'tone deaf', but in practice this condition is very rare. The evidence suggests that most people can learn to sing if they are keen enough and willing to practice regularly.

An interesting study, by Peter Q. Pfordresher and Steven Brown reported in Scientific American magazine in 2008, attempted to discover why some people are terrible singers. The researchers discovered that most of the bad singers in their study were not literally tone deaf. In fact, they were just as good at detecting the difference between notes of various frequencies as the good singers. But when they tried to produce the notes themselves, they were far worse. The researchers were able to rule out poor memory or hearing difficulties as potential causes for this.

This study suggests that most bad singers are still able to appreciate good music. What they don't have is the ability to transfer this ability to singing in tune themselves, probably due to a lack of co-ordination. They are like a beginner golfer who can see the ball on the tee and swing their club, but misses the ball every time.

Hydrochloric acid is a powerful chemical that will burn you badly if it gets on your skin. So why doesn't it burn through the container it's stored in?

The answer is that, for this to happen, a chemical reaction would need to occur where the acid meets the container wall, making it dissolve. The acid would then progressively work its way through to the outside.

Acids are essentially chemical compounds that are happy to transfer a proton to another atom. So provided you have a material that either has no sites where protons can be accepted, or on which protons have no structural effect, there's no problem.

Hydrochloric acid can be stored safely in a variety of materials. Glass or ceramic (porcelain) are good choices. These substances are based on silicon and oxygen. While the oxygen atoms on the surface can accept the odd proton, this has no effect because it doesn't weaken the overall structure.

Plastics such as polyethylene or polypropylene are also fine. These substances have virtually no binding sites for protons, so nothing happens.

Metals would be a bad choice, however. Not only will hydrochloric acid react with most metals, gases including the toxic chlorine will be released as well. That's why you'll never see hydrochloric acid sold in tins.

69 What is the imprint that is left in your vision after you look at a bright light?

The area at the back of your eyes on which images are formed is called the retina. The retina is lined with millions of light-sensitive cells which, when stimulated, send messages to the brain. This is what we interpret as vision.

Different cells in the retina are sensitive to different wavelengths of light, so according to which ones are transmitting, we interpret what we see as a particular color.

When we look at a very bright object, the light-sensitive cells of the retina are over-stimulated. For a few seconds they are unable to transmit any new information to the brain, and continue to transmit the 'old' information until they recover. Hence, we continue to see an after-image of the light, even if we close our eyes.

If you look at a specific color of bright light, only cells sensitive to that particular color are over-stimulated. If you look at a bright red light, for example, the cells responding to that wavelength will be temporarily knocked out. If you then look at a piece of white paper, you will still stimulate the blue- and yellow-sensitive cells in the retina. Because the red cells are out of action, however, the white paper will appear green (a combination of blue and yellow).

Warning: Avoid doing this too often or you could permanently damage your eyes. In particular, you should NEVER stare directly at the sun.

This is another of those questions where we have to start by saying that nobody knows for sure. There is no shortage of theories, however.

The great psychologist Sigmund Freud thought dreams were a form of wish-fulfillment, in which people acted out their deepest wishes. People whose dreams were largely boring, however, found this explanation hard to believe!

One modern theory compares our mind to a computer to account for dreams. According to this theory, dreams serve as a way of 'de-cluttering' the mind, much like the clean-up operations in a computer. They help us sort out and process the day's events, and prepare our mind so that it is fresh for the next day.

Another model proposes that dreams function as a form of therapy. In this theory, the dreamer is playing out the day's events in different ways, perhaps trying to make sense of difficult emotional situations, in a safe environment.

Even though we may not remember our dreams, they appear to be essential to our health and well-being. Studies have shown that if people are deprived of dreams (which can happen as a side-effect of using certain drugs), the result can be mental illness and hallucinations. This can happen as a result of dream deprivation even if you are getting enough sleep otherwise.

Why do raisins bob up and down in a glass of champagne?

A raisin dropped in a glass of fresh champagne will bob up and down continually from the bottom of the glass to the top – try it out yourself and see!

The reason this happens is that the wrinkles on the raisins get bubbles of carbon dioxide gas from the drink stuck to them. When enough bubbles accumulate to lift the weight of the raisin, it rises to the surface. There, some of the bubbles escape into the air, and the raisin, which is denser than the champagne, sinks back to the bottom. The cycle then starts over again.

The effect will last longer if you put the champagne in a sealed container such as a jam jar, as less carbon dioxide will be able to escape.

If you don't have any raisins to hand, some other small objects will work just as well: mothballs or pieces of uncooked pasta, for example. The key is that they are dense enough to sink in water, able to trap air bubbles on their surface, light enough to be buoyed to the surface by the bubbles, and won't dissolve in the liquid. If you don't want to waste good champagne trying this out – and who could blame you? – soda or any carbonated drink will produce a similar effect.

Why do you weigh less in the morning than at night?

It's quite true that people weigh less in the morning than at night. The reason is mainly down to water loss.

First of all, every time you breathe out, you lose a certain amount of water vapor from your lungs. Water lost this way amounts to around 350 ml/12 oz per day at normal temperatures. This amount of water would weigh about 350 grams.

The skin loses another 350 ml/12 oz of water every day to insensible perspiration (that which you do not notice as liquid water but evaporates directly into the air).

The sweat you do notice is lost at a rate in proportion to the surrounding temperature and your level of activity. At normal temperatures and with little activity, as at night, you would lose approximately 100 ml of water per day by this means. In warm weather or a heatwave, obviously, you could lose a lot more than this.

And finally, if you have to use the bathroom during the night, the effect will be still more water loss.

The net effect of these three factors means that overnight your body could easily lose a kilogram or more in weight. A good reason to have a hearty breakfast.

73 Why do you get the urge to urinate when you hear the sound of running water?

If you've had this happen, you're not alone! It's a very common experience.

It's actually an example of something called classical conditioning. If you've ever studied psychology, you may have heard of a researcher called Pavlov, who rang a bell every time he fed his dogs. The dogs came to associate the bell with food, and when it was rung they produced more saliva (a secretion needed to make food easier to swallow and digest). After a while, this happened even if no food was around.

Here's how it works with the sound of running water. Urination is controlled by two sphincters (cut-off valves) in the urinary tract. One is voluntary and the other is involuntary. Once a certain amount of urine has collected in our bladder, the involuntary sphincter opens, leaving full control to the voluntary sphincter. This is when we feel the urge to pass water, though of course we normally wait till the moment is right before opening the voluntary sphincter!

The sound of running water is something our body has come to associate with urinating, as the two often happen together. When we hear running water, therefore, the involuntary sphincter opens, and we get the urge to urinate, even if not much urine has collected. It's a conditioned reflex, and not one we have any conscious control over.

Some mushrooms (or more accurately fungi) do indeed grow in circles. Myths ascribe these rings to fairies, witches, dragons, and so on, but the true explanation is natural rather than supernatural.

They grow in circles because the mushroom is just the fruiting body of a large organism (correctly named a mycelium) that is mostly underground. In simple terms, the mushroom is the 'flower' of a plant that exists mostly as a massive underground root system.

The part of the mushroom that is underground is circular because it grew from a single spore and then spread out in all directions from there. Just as the canopy of a tree is round, so the mycelium of a fungus is roughly circular.

When conditions are right, normally in the autumn, the mycelium sends up mushrooms on the youngest growth. Because the youngest growth is at the outer edge of the mycelium, the mushrooms appear in a circle. As the mycelium grows it continues to widen, so the mushrooms appear in a larger circle every year.

Of course, it may well be true that goblins and fairies use these rings for their midnight parties, but they aren't responsible for them growing that way in the first place.

Many people experience this reaction – the chances are that if you don't do it yourself, you'll know someone who does.

There is actually a name for the phenomenon – it's called 'photic' sneezing. It happens to a lot of people, especially when they come out of a dark place like a movie theater and into bright sunlight.

The reason it occurs is because we have nerves close to the eyes and nose that, when stimulated or irritated, send a signal to the brain to cause the sneeze reflex. In some people who have particularly sensitive nerves there, a bright light will stimulate the sneeze reflex nerve, causing us to sneeze.

Sensitivity varies a lot. Some people only have this happen when they go straight from a dark room into bright sunlight, while other unfortunate individuals suffer much more. Adam Sneed, an Arizona State University student, aged 21, even gets sneezing fits when the light on his cell phone comes on.

It's usually genetic too, so if you are a photic sneezer, there is a good chance that other members of your family are as well. Geneticists, displaying a healthy dose of humor, refer to this as ACHOO syndrome, which stands for Autosomal dominant Compelling Helio-Ophthalmic Outburst. And that's enough to make anyone sneeze.

76 Why do wet things smell more than dry ones?

A classic example of this is dogs. And the short answer is evaporation.

In the case of dogs, they carry all sorts of potentially smelly substances around with them. But we don't notice them when the dog is dry, because all these malodorous molecules are locked up inside the dry dirt.

When the dog gets wet, though, these interesting substances get the chance to dissolve in the water. Some of the water then evaporates, taking the dissolved molecules with it – and some arrive in our nostrils, where we can savor their distinctive aroma. Time for Rover's bath.

77 Why do boomerangs come back?

When you throw a boomerang correctly, it starts to spin as soon as you release it. This causes air to flow rapidly over the airfoils, which creates the lift that makes the boomerang fly.

Because the boomerang is also moving forward, the arm spinning into the direction of flight creates more lift than the arm spinning away. This means there is more lift on one side of the spinning boomerang than the other.

Any spinning object is subject to gyroscopic precession. Simply put, this means any attempt to move a spinning object is translated at right angles. With a boomerang, precession makes it turn left, causing it to fly back in a circle.

78 Can a person swing 360 degrees on a swing set?

It's a question we all wonder about as kids – if you swing hard enough, could you go all the way round? There's even a rumor that if you do this, you will turn yourself inside-out.

Perhaps fortunately, then, the answer is 'no'. If you're on a chain or rope swing, it's simply impossible to go much beyond the horizontal.

To understand why, think of a swing as a sort of pendulum. When you reach the highest point, you have potential energy but no kinetic (movement) energy. At the bottom, you're moving fastest and have the most kinetic energy, but no potential energy.

Getting yourself to swing further involves raising your center of gravity by 'pulling yourself up' the chain at the end of the arc. This gives you a bit more potential energy, meaning you end up moving faster (more kinetic energy) at the bottom. But if you get to the horizontal, this doesn't work, as pulling yourself up the chain doesn't give you any extra height.

The other reason it can't be done is that once you get past the horizontal, on the downswing you won't initially descend in a neat arc but, due to gravity, a more direct drop. This causes the chain to loosen then jerk tight again, which wastes some energy. These two factors together mean it's impossible to swing much higher than horizontal.

79 Why does your voice sound better when you sing in the bathroom?

Most of us think our singing voice sounds better in the bathroom, though someone else listening might not always agree!

The main reason is that bathrooms are usually quite small and have lots of hard, smooth surfaces that reflect sound back to us. As a result, you hear a lot of short echoes that harmonize with your own voice. Technically this is called reverberation, or 'reverb' for short. In recording studios they have special software that can add this effect electronically, but in your bathroom you get it automatically for free!

The blurring of your voice by reverberation has another benefit. It helps even out variations in pitch, which is useful if you aren't always quite in tune. Karaoke bars usually add electronic reverb to the voices of novice singers for this reason.

There may also be other reasons your voice sounds better in the bathroom. You are in a relaxed situation. The steam from the shower can loosen tension in your body and add hydration to your voice. And you are also less tense because you are alone and no-one is judging your performance.

For all these reasons the bathroom can be a great place to practice your singing. Just don't expect to be asked for an encore by other family members when you emerge.

How do lasers cut through things? Aren't they just light?

Lasers are electrical devices that do indeed produce powerful beams of light. However, laser light has some unusual properties.

One of these is that it's all a single color. Unlike the light from an ordinary lightbulb, which is a jumble of different wavelengths, all the light from a laser is one specific frequency.

Laser light is also coherent. That means as well as being a single frequency, all the waves emitted by a laser are in phase with one another. It is this coherence of laser light that makes holograms possible.

And finally, laser light can be focused into a tight beam which does not diverge nearly as much as (say) a flashlight beam.

It is these special properties of laser light that make it suitable for cutting through things. Cutting lasers use infrared light that is actually invisible to the human eye – it's the heat you feel when you stand near a space heater. This form of radiation is ideal for delivering energy into a material in such a way that it heats and then cuts it very precisely. The laser sends high-energy infrared light in a very tight beam into the material concerned.

As mentioned, infrared light is invisible and so when such lasers cut, all you see is the hot spot on the material. It's not like the James Bond film Goldfinger, where you see a red beam gradually approaching our prostrate hero.

Winds are caused because the sun heats the planet differently, and over vast areas. As an area warms up, the air expands, causing a pressure change. Wind is simply high pressure air moving towards a low pressure region, to balance things out.

The closer the high and low pressure areas are together, the stronger the winds will be. On weather maps, lines showing air of the same pressure are called 'isobars' and they are usually labeled with their pressure value in millibars (mb). The closer these lines are together, the stronger will be the winds.

Wind can also be regarded as a way the atmosphere moves excess heat around. All wind is, directly or indirectly, helping to transport heat. It is either taking it away from the surface of the earth to higher up, or from warm regions (usually the tropics) to cooler regions (usually the higher latitudes).

In practice, it is more complicated than this, as airflows are diverted by the rotation of the earth, giving rise to hurricanes and other spiral storm systems. The uneven distribution of land and sea and the presence of mountain belts further complicate the picture, as do random events such as volcanic eruptions.

All of this means that the wind and weather in one year is never an exact replica of the previous one. At least, it always gives us something to talk about.

82 Why doesn't the Olympic flame cast a shadow?

If you've watched the opening ceremony at the Olympic Games, you may have noticed that while the Olympic torch and the athlete holding it cast shadows, the flame itself doesn't.

This happens even though the torch is producing a bright flame you can't see through. So why is there no shadow?

The answer is that the opening ceremony normally takes place at night, under artificial lights. When the light from a spotlight is blocked, for instance by an athlete's body, the area behind him or her will appear darker because less light is able to reach it directly. This is what we call a shadow.

A torch flame is unusual, however, because it is also a source of light. It is obviously not as bright as a spotlight, but then again it is a lot closer to the ground. The net effect, then, is that the light emitted from the flame compensates for the light from the spotlight that is blocked. As a result, we don't see any shadow from the flame, or perhaps just a very pale, ghostly one.

You can reproduce this effect yourself by lighting a candle in a dark room and shining a flashlight on it. You will see a clear shadow of the candle itself, but hardly any from the flame.

83 Why is pain easier to bear if you shout and scream?

For most people, shouting and screaming in response to pain is an instinctive reaction.

There are various reasons for this. One is that human beings are basically social animals. Shouting and screaming serve to tell other members of our tribe that we are hurt and need help. They also warn of a possible danger from whatever is making us scream (bear, leopard, snake, etc.).

Screaming may also serve to make pain easier to bear by giving us something else to focus on. By doing this, we try to 'drown out' the pain messages arriving in our brain and replace them with sound messages instead.

And finally, shouting and screaming helps to mobilize our fight-or-flight instinct. It makes us produce the hormone adrenalin, which speeds up our heart rate and prepares us for immediate action, either by fighting whatever is causing our pain or running to escape from it.

Of course sometimes – like when we're at the dentist – shouting and screaming isn't very helpful or appropriate. In these circumstances, a shot of anesthetic to numb the pain is usually a much better, and more dignified, option.

The odd colors and shapes many people see when they close their eyes are called phosphenes.

They are believed to be caused by the random firing of cells in the retina and other parts of the visual system.

You can also produce phosphenes deliberately by rubbing your closed eyes. This stimulates the cells of the retina to fire, and the resulting nerve impulses are interpreted as vision by the brain. Pressure phosphenes, as they are called, can carry on briefly after the rubbing stops and the eyes are opened, allowing the phosphenes to be seen over your natural vision.

One pressure phosphene that works for most people is to press gently against the side of your closed eye. You will then see a ring of colored light on the opposite side. This phenomenon was first described by no less than Sir Isaac Newton, who first explained the laws of gravity.

Phosphenes have also been created artificially by electrical stimulation of the brain, and by exposure to strong magnetic fields. In recent years, researchers have successfully developed electrical devices that stimulate phosphenes, to restore vision to people blinded through accidents.

Of course, if you start seeing pink elephants or large white rabbits when you close your eyes, it might be time to see the doctor.

A rainbow is one of the wonders of the natural world. It is caused by sunlight being refracted by millions of raindrops.

In effect, each raindrop in a rainbow acts like a tiny prism. Light entering the raindrops from the sun is split into its component colors. This happens because colors of higher frequencies (e.g. violet) are refracted or 'bent' more within each drop than lower frequency colors (e.g. red).

We see bands of color in a rainbow because all the raindrops in that part of the sky are refracting light of a particular color into our eye. This happens because most of the light is coming from the sun directly, so the light entering the raindrops is coming in at the same angle. If the sun isn't visible, the light is diffused and comes from all different directions, so we don't see a rainbow.

There are various ways you can create your own rainbow, but perhaps the easiest is by using a waterhose on a sunny day. Place your finger over the nozzle to create a fine spray between where you are standing and the sun. If you look into the spray, once you've found the correct angle, you will be rewarded by your very own rainbow.

86 Why can't we get thinner by thinking, if our brains burn calories?

It would be great if we really could 'think ourselves thin', but unfortunately it's very unlikely to happen.

It's true that the brain burns up a lot of energy – around 20% of your total calories, which is a lot for a relatively small organ. However, this energy comes from sugars (and specifically glucose) rather than fat.

Fat molecules can't be broken down into glucose, and it's glucose that powers the nerve cells in your brain. Fats can only be broken down and used by the brain if no glucose is available – so you would literally need to be starving before your brain started burning fat. In that case, the last thing you would want is to get any thinner, of course!

The other reason thinking doesn't make us thinner is that it represents a very small percentage of the total energy used in the brain. It requires quite a lot of energy just to keep the nerve cells ready to fire, and there is also a large amount of activity going on in the brain which is not directly involved in conscious awareness. So the brain is constantly using energy, even if we're not aware of it.

Nothing for it unfortunately – if you want to lose weight, it's time to head off to the gym.

87 Why does switching off the lights when leaving a room not always save money?

You might think switching off lights when you leave a room would always save money, because you are using less electricity.

That's true, of course, but with modern fluorescent lights, there are two slight complications. One is that every time you switch them on and off, it shortens their life slightly. And second, when you first switch on a fluorescent light, there is a brief power surge.

Nonetheless, overall you will still save a lot more money by turning lights off when you don't need them. A good rule of thumb is to leave fluorescent lights on if you're planning to leave the room for less than five minutes, but otherwise switch them off.

88 How do they put bubbles in chocolate?

Tiny bubbles of gas (generally nitrogen or a mixture of nitrogen and carbon dioxide) are passed through liquid chocolate. The chocolate is then cooled in a vacuum, causing the gas bubbles trapped inside the chocolate to expand. The result is a sort of chocolate foam, with evenly distributed bubbles and a honeycomb-like texture.

Mmm, delicious!

89 Who invented time?

It's a moot point whether time was invented or discovered.

Some say that time was invented by human beings to give order to their lives. Others regard time as part of the fundamental structure of the universe. In the latter view, nobody invented time, they just discovered it.

Prehistoric man probably first became aware of time and the need to measure it when he noticed that certain events occurred at regular intervals – the changing of the seasons, for example. This regularity was important for planning farming, sacred feasts, long journeys, and so on. As a result, our early ancestors began to come up with primitive methods for measuring time.

One of the earliest time-measurement devices before clocks and watches was the hourglass. This was made of two glass bulbs with a narrow glass neck between them. When the hourglass is turned upside down, sand particles stream from the top to the bottom – and when the top bulb is empty, an hour has passed. Today's egg-timers are modern versions of the hourglass.

Einstein (yes, him again) proposed that time is relative. In particular, it goes more slowly in higher gravitational fields, a phenomenon called gravitational time dilation. According to Einstein's theory, time cannot exist without space being present as well. So before the universe was created in the Big Bang, time didn't exist either. And if you think that's a hard concept to get your head around, join the club.

The short answer is that nobody knows.

It's not impossible. Einstein's General Theory of Relativity is the best explanation we have at present of the nature of space and time. Einstein's equations and the theory itself do not prohibit the idea of time travel. Although there have been many attempts since Einstein to demonstrate that traveling back in time is impossible, nobody has so far succeeded in proving this. We all travel into the future every day of course!

On the other hand, most physicists agree that time travel is extremely unlikely. There are huge practical and theoretical obstacles. On the practical side, the most likely mechanism for allowing time travel is a localized distortion in space-time, otherwise known as a wormhole. Traveling through a wormhole is likely to be difficult (and dangerous)!

The biggest theoretical obstacle is known as the time-travel paradox. If someone goes back in time and does something to prevent their own existence, how can this be possible? The classic example is the time traveler who kills his grandfather before his own father is born. Many science-fiction authors have had fun exploring this paradox.

In addition, if time travel really is possible, we should be inundated with visitors from the future, come to check out their ancestors. As far as anyone knows, this isn't the case.

This is, of course, a hypothetical question. Only particles with no mass, such as photons, can go at the speed of light.

Einstein's theory of relativity shows that as an object with mass (such as a car) approaches the speed of light, the amount of energy needed to accelerate it further increases, so that an infinite amount would be needed to reach light speed.

But let's assume you're in a very special car that can go at *almost* the speed of light. In that case, if you switch on the headlights, from your perspective they will come on as normal and light the way ahead. Einstein's theory states that the speed of light is constant, and it doesn't change just because you are traveling faster.

From the perspective of a stationary observer, however, the beam of light will appear to come out of the headlights really slowly. There is only one explanation for this. Time is passing at different rates for you and the observer. What seems a very short time for you in the speeding car appears a very long time for the observer. This explains why the headlight appears to operate normally for you, yet to the outside observer seems to be in slow motion. This is what we mean when we say that time and space are relative.

And yes, this is another of those mind-blowing aspects of relativity.

92 What effect does dark matter have on our solar system?

Dark matter is a term for material in the universe which we can't see but can tell exists because of its gravitational effect on other objects in the universe. Scientists believe that more than 90 per cent of the total mass of the universe may be dark matter.

Dark matter is unlikely to have much effect on our solar system, because (in cosmic terms) the solar system is simply too small. So far, all the evidence about dark matter suggests that it only affects big objects, like galaxies and galaxy clusters.

Most scientists believe dark matter is streaming through our solar system all the time as we move through the universe. It's very hard to detect, however, because it seldom interacts with normal matter. Its particles are therefore described as 'weakly interacting massive particles' or WIMPs for short (yes, truly!).

Scientists have not yet been able to observe WIMPs directly, though they are following two lines of inquiry. First, although weakly interacting, it is thought that on very rare occasions a dark matter particle may collide with a particle of normal matter. Scientists are trying to observe the recoil in underground laboratories. The other approach is to try to produce a WIMP in a collider experiment, such as the Large Hadron Collider in Switzerland.

But overall, if you want something to worry about, dark matter engulfing our solar system should probably be very low on your list.

93 Why does your heartbeat change with music?

There's no doubt music can affect our heart rate. In one study at the University of Oxford, young people were monitored to see how their heart rate and blood pressure changed while listening to different kinds of music.

The study found that listeners' bodies responded directly to the tempo of the music. Heart rate increased when listening to music with a fast tempo, and decreased with music with a slow tempo.

The style of the music had some effect but didn't appear nearly as important as tempo. Rap and heavy rock music increased heart rate the most, while classical and reggae slowed it the most.

Nobody is sure why this happens. Part of the explanation may be that if we find music exciting or unpleasant, our body makes more adrenalin, the fight-or-flight hormone that raises our heart rate. There is some evidence for this, as if someone strongly dislikes a certain type of music, their heart rate goes up when they hear it, regardless of tempo.

This doesn't explain why some types of music can lower heart rate however. It seems that slow-tempo music somehow acts through our nervous system to slow our pulse but the exact way this works still isn't clear.

Overall, though, if you want to slow down your heart rate and lower your blood pressure, listening to some slow-tempo music – as long as you don't hate it – is a good way of doing this.

94 Where does all the rubber lost from tires go?

That's a very good question. One British study found that about 10 to 20 per cent of a tire's total weight is worn off during its lifetime, which works out to about 58,000 tons a year in the UK alone. The figure in the US is estimated to be around 650,000 tons per year.

Tires are a mixture of materials, mostly synthetic and natural rubbers, but also including oil, sulfur, steel, and other chemicals.

As people drive around, and especially as they corner and brake, the tires of their vehicles rub against the road, and some of the rubber wears off. Heavier particles are left on the roads and pavements, while smaller particles go into the air, adding to atmospheric pollution.

Rubber in the air is bad news for people with a latex allergy. Somewhere between 1 and 6 per cent of the population have some sensitivity to latex, which can result in rashes, inflammation, asthma, and worse. Even if you're not allergic, excessive exposure to fine particles in the air from tires can lead to reduced lung capacity, bronchitis, asthma, heart disease and worse.

If you're a driver, one way you can minimize the amount of rubber lost from your tires is by ensuring that they are always inflated to the recommended pressure. This will improve the mileage you get as well, so you can save money AND help save the environment.

95 Why does your brain hurt even when there are no pain receptors?

There are indeed no pain receptors in the brain. This is why people undergoing brain surgery can be alert, with anesthetic administered only locally to the scalp.

If this is so, how do we experience the pain of headaches and migraines, especially those that seem to come from a specific point inside our head, and throb and radiate from that point?

Firstly, while the brain itself may have no pain sensors, other parts of the head do. These include muscles, blood vessels and sinuses. Problems with any of these are often the cause of a headache. Even problems in the brain, such as tumors, create pain indirectly, by pressing against structures than can register pain.

There is also the phenomenon called referred pain. When we cannot correctly interpret pain signals from nerves serving parts of the body we are unfamiliar with, we may interpret them as headaches. Many headaches fall into this category, and one thing they all have in common is that the pain receptors involved are not part of the brain tissue.

Nobody is sure what causes migraine headaches, but current opinion is that they do not originate in the brain itself but from inflamed meninges, the membranes that surround and nourish the brain.

Of course, even though it may not originate in your brain itself, that doesn't stop a headache being a pain in the neck!

96 Why do you vomit when you over-exercise?

During exercise blood is shunted to the muscles, so that they can get all the oxygen they need and waste products such as lactic acid are speedily removed.

Because there is only so much blood available in the body, it is diverted from other organs such as the stomach. During heavy exercise, digestion stops. Whatever is in the stomach just sits there with nothing to do and nowhere to go. If it's jostled around long enough, it stimulates the vomiting reflex.

For this reason, it's best to avoid eating directly before a vigorous workout. Much better for all concerned to wait and have your meal afterwards.

97 Can an opera singer really shatter a wine glass with her voice?

The theory is simple enough. Every piece of glass has a natural resonant frequency. If a person sings that exact note, the glass will start vibrating at that frequency, and eventually shake itself to bits.

In practice, though, it's not as simple as this. The singer would have to hit exactly the right note at a suitably high volume, and even then the glass would need to have some microscopic flaws.

Until 2005, there was no documented proof of a singer ever doing this. Then the US TV show MythBusters recruited rock singer Jamie Vendera to give it his best shot. He tried twelve wine glasses, before finally stumbling on one that shattered.

M ost races – animal and mechanical, as well as human – are run in an anticlockwise direction. Nobody is sure of the exact reason.

One popular myth is that it's a custom started by the Greeks which everyone has followed since. In fact, evidence suggests that the ancient Greeks raced in a clockwise direction.

Most track races nowadays are run anticlockwise because of an international agreement stipulating the direction. This is meant to make it easier to set up timing equipment across different venues.

As a matter of interest, in very long track races (over 12 hours), the directions are periodically changed during the race. The outside leg does more work, so the direction is switched to reduce fatigue.

There are two reasons for this. One is that pigeons don't fledge (leave the nest) until they are pretty much adult-sized.

And second, they grow up extremely fast, due to a high-fat, high-protein diet of crop milk produced by both parents. Most species of pigeons rear their young to independence in under three weeks.

Baby pigeons that have just fledged are typically as large, and sometimes larger, than the parents.
You may be able to recognize them by the shape of their beaks, which are slightly flatter and wider than an adult's.

Also, for the first week or two after leaving the nest, the feathers around the base of their beak are bristly and lay back along the face.

Black is the color – or more correctly absence of color – you get when looking at something that doesn't give off any light. The night sky looks black to us because there is hardly any visible light coming from the areas you are looking at.

It's different during the day, because then there is a lot of light coming from all over the sky, mainly from sunlight being reflected within the atmosphere. At night, however, the sun is hidden, and during this time we are looking straight through the atmosphere into outer space.

So why does so little visible light come from space? If the universe is infinite, surely you should be able to travel in any direction forever and eventually hit a star? Yet we don't see light from stars everywhere we look. This puzzle is known as Olbers' Paradox, after an amateur astronomer named Heinrich Wilhelm Olbers, who described it in 1823.

The most widely accepted explanation for Olbers' Paradox today assumes that the universe began with a 'Big Bang' an estimated 13.7 billion years ago. The further away a star is from the Earth, the longer the light from it takes to reach us. The assumption is that in areas of the night sky which look black to us, the distance of the invisible background is so immense that no ray of light from it has yet had time to reach us.

And if you find that pretty mind-blowing, don't worry, we do as well.

A note on spelling:
Since this edition is sold worldwide we have
used American English spellings throughout.